Contents

D0950506

1. Your To-Do List

2. Next Steps

STARTING OVER

Dave Ramsey's Post-Bankruptcy
SURVIVAL GUIDE

LAMPO
PRESS
THE LAMPO GROUP, INC.

Editors: Richard Speight and Darcie Clemen
Cover and interior design: Chris Sandlin

ISBN: 9-781934-629772

OUR MISSION IS TO **EMPOWER** AND
GIVE HOPE TO EVERYONE FROM
THE FINANCIALLY SECURE TO THE
FINANCIALLY DISTRESSED.

—Dave Ramsey

Introduction: Dan's Story

I'm Dan. I head Dave Ramsey's Debtor Education team, which may seem odd since I have never filed for bankruptcy protection. Well, it's not odd at all. The advice and recommendations in this book reflect the life experience and teachings of Dave Ramsey, who—along with his wife, Sharon—did file for bankruptcy protection more than two decades ago.

When they walked away from the courthouse that last time, Dave and Sharon had no idea what to do next to rebuild their financial and family lives. They turned to prayer, dedication, and a lot of hard work, and eventually they created the *Financial Peace University* program. That program has been changing lives and spreading hope for more than two decades.

The subject here is not filing for bankruptcy. You've already done that. This book is about what you do next, after the judge's gavel has come down for the last time in your case. In that respect, I am the perfect person to head this program. Like Dave, I had to rebuild almost everything.

In 2006 I moved my family from Virginia to Tennessee to take a job with a small, but growing, company. We bought our first house, carried some debt, and drove two nice cars that came complete with monthly payments.

I was introduced to Dave Ramsey and *Financial Peace University* for the first time in 2007, when my wife and I went through the program. We were hooked from the beginning. We saved a baby emergency fund, cut up our credit cards, and began chipping away at debt using Dave's "debt snowball."

My company furnished a truck for me, so I sold my car for the exact amount owed on the note. We jointly decided to keep paying the note on the "nicer" car, which my wife got to drive, of course—isn't that required by law?

In 2009 I was laid off without notice and given several weeks of severance pay. The company truck was taken back and given to the CEO. A colleague drove me home. I was depressed, scared, embarrassed, and angry all at the same time.

After a period of pouting, crying, stomping, and shouting, I realized that if things were going to get better, I would have to take charge and make that happen. I went back and reread most of the book *Financial Peace*. Thank God we were already living the Dave Ramsey principles.

I had exactly $1,900 to spend on a used car. I finally found a small Mazda with 180,000 miles on it. The engine checked out fine. There were cosmetic issues, of course, and problems with the electric locks and other features, but it would get me from point A to point B, which was all I needed.

They were asking $2,200. I offered $1,800 cash, and they took it. I drove it straight to a local pizza place and asked if they needed delivery drivers. I started the next day. That put food on our table. I worked two other part-time jobs and painted homes on the side during the next six months, so we were able to get by while I searched for a great new career.

As it turned out, I was able to find a dream job heading up Dave Ramsey's Debtor Education program. And I have learned a lot from my 300-plus teammates, most of whom have fought the same battles and are learning to win with money the *Financial Peace University* way.

It's been three years now, and I still do odd jobs when my schedule permits so we can pay down the last of our debt that much faster. And yes, I'm still driving that Mazda. For the record, it now has 256,000 miles on it. Also, my wife still drives the nicer car, only it's paid off. She says it drives even better without the stupid payments.

During those six months I juggled as many as four jobs at a time. It was not fun. But that sacrifice paid off big time. We were living like no one else during that time, but soon we will be completely debt-free and able to really live like no one else.

So don't tell me it can't be done or it won't work. Don't tell that to anyone here at Financial Peace Plaza (yes, there really is such a place). We know better. We're doing it.

—Dan Rolfson
Vice President, Dave Ramsey's Debtor Education

Your Fresh Start

How many times have you heard those words since you began the bankruptcy process? Did they make you feel hopeful? Were they so routinely used that they lost their significance? Did you really understand the opportunity presented to you?

We'd like to help you do that.

When you walked out of your lawyer's office that last time, you probably felt better than you expected you would. That's what usually happens. You had been under the care of skilled professionals who were concerned about your welfare, who knew what they were doing, and whose goal was to secure for you every positive result achievable in your case.

Dave Ramsey's memory of the pain and stress that led to his personal bankruptcy and the relief he felt after his discharge are both quite vivid almost three decades after his experience. The gut-wrenching, marriage-twisting trauma of being on the brink of financial ruin with no one to blame but himself definitely took a terrible toll. But his discharge lifted a tremendous weight off of him, and when it was done he and his wife Sharon were still together, facing their own fresh start.

On the morning after their last trip to court, Dave remembers that he and Sharon asked each other the question that faces all discharged bankrupt debtors.

"What do we do next?"

What Dave did next—live a debt-free life and teach his God-and-grandma philosophy to millions—is a part of history. But in reality there was no immediate answer to the challenging question they posed at the breakfast table that morning. They were on their own, without guidelines, instructions, solutions, a plan, or knowledgeable mentors to whom they could turn.

Now, decades later, Dave has challenged his Bankruptcy Debtor Education team to fill this void that he and thousands of other discharged debtors have faced by producing this book.

A fresh start really is what Congress intended when the current Bankruptcy Act's predecessor was signed into law in 1938. Helping debtors achieve that lofty goal remains the underlying principle of the bankruptcy process to this very day.

So why do many debtors fail to experience the kind of fresh start they've wished for and dreamed about? More importantly, how can you avoid becoming discouraged and disheartened? How can you keep from ending up where you started—broke, in debt, angry, and disappointed?

Over the days, weeks, and months following their discharge, Dave and Sharon's answer came into sharp focus and became completely clear: it was up to them to define their own fresh start. By the same token, in your case it's up to you.

We want to help. At Dave Ramsey's Debtor Education, our mission is to offer genuine hope and as much practical assistance as possible.

Let's begin by understanding and accepting a simple fact that most bankrupt debtors miss. A fresh start isn't a gift. It is an opportunity.

Your discharge has left you with a lot more work to do. But the bankruptcy process cleared away the major obstacles that kept you from moving forward and changing your life for the better. That's not just good news; it's great news. You can achieve a fresh start for yourself and your family, and you have the power to make that fresh start whatever you want it to be!

The following chapters are designed to deal with the fundamental question, "What do we do next?" From issues of absolute necessity and immediate priority all the way through broader choices, options, and opportunities, we will try to teach you the how and why of personal finance as it applies to those who, like you, have just come through a life-changing experience.

We're going to get pretty specific in the first part of the book by offering you a literal "to-do" list, which, if followed in sequence, will lead you toward financial peace. How do we know that's what will happen? Because this list is based upon the proven principles of Dave Ramsey's *Financial Peace University*. Millions have freed themselves from the bondage of debt and have become financially secure and generous people by beginning their journey in that program and by following through with tenacity and determination.

Tenacity and determination are literally all you have to bring with you as you begin this journey. We will provide the tools. You are holding the instruction manual in your hands.

We're excited about this opportunity to bring you the kind of help and hope that has characterized Dave Ramsey's life for the last twenty-five years, ever since he sat down at a folding table in his dining room and began scratching out his life's goals on a legal pad. Dave and Sharon really did experience a fresh start. They stuck together and stuck with it and made it happen. Now we're asking you to stay with us all the way through this book, soak it in, and make these principles part of who you are. Make your fresh start a winner.

You'll be glad you did.

Questions and More Questions

The wave of adrenaline that carried you home from the courthouse will eventually slow to a trickle, and reality will set in. Maybe it already has. The life that is spread out before you may contain more questions than answers, some of which may keep you awake at night.

The lawyers who helped pull you back from the edge of disaster would like nothing better than to keep holding your hand and guiding you and your loved ones gently into the future, but they don't have that luxury. So they have set you free to continue on your own.

The paralegals and other members of their staff—kind, patient men and women who untangled the mess, handled the details, shared your pain, and cheered you on—have now turned their attention to doing the same for other clients. You are no longer on their radar. You can call on them in emergencies, of course. But it's time for you to work on your own financial future.

By the way, if you haven't done so already, you might want to express your gratitude to those individuals who helped make your fresh start possible.

You are on your own, but you aren't alone. Your concerns are not new. There are thousands who have shared your experience, and many more will come along in the future. Here at Financial Peace Plaza, the site of Dave Ramsey's radio show and the home of all his programs, we've been asked every possible question more times than we can count. Here are some of the ones we hear most often from bankruptcy filers signing up for Dave Ramsey's Debtor Education course:

- Will my bankruptcy haunt me, label me, and keep me from improving myself?

- Will I find work or improve my situation enough to not go into debt again?

- Will I ever be able to buy a house again with a bankruptcy on my record?

- Will I be able to keep the house I reaffirmed?

- If not, should I walk away or try to negotiate?

- Is a short sale something that would work well in my case?

- How will I be able to rent when my credit score is in the toilet?

- How can I improve my credit score without borrowing money again?

- Did I do right keeping that car with its huge monthly payments?

- I've got to have a car. How can I get one without financing it?

- How can I make a major purchase without putting it on a credit card?

- Someone I really care about wants me to co-sign a note. Should I do that?

- How can I build an emergency fund when I'm living paycheck to paycheck?

- With all I've been through, aren't I entitled to enjoy the good life for a while?

These are truly difficult issues, and there are no easy answers. Anxious days do lie ahead. We can't change that, and you can't avoid it.

Yet there's another set of questions even heavier with emotion— questions born from your decision to declare bankruptcy. Again, there's nothing new under the sun. Thousands have asked:

- Did I do the right thing?
- How can I avoid making the same mistakes again?
- Will my marriage survive?
- Is my spouse terribly disappointed in me?
- Do my children see me differently?
- Do my friends and fellow workers think less of me?
- Will these negative feelings ever end?
- What is the most important thing to do right now?

When we offer an answer, it will be based on decades of experience on the front lines of this battlefield. When we have no answer, we'll try to direct you to the best possible source. At all times, our objective will be to respond with compassion and offer excellence.

The following sections are a comprehensive to-do list for you to begin working on immediately after your discharge. The more items you check off, the better your chance at financial peace and prosperity. Not everything on this list will be required of every discharged debtor. Check off the items that do not require action in your case, but be aware of them. You will know that you are on the right path, doing things in the right order.

Your To-Do List

Secure Your Four Walls

The Four Walls are food, shelter and utilities, clothing, and transportation. Before you begin traveling the road to financial peace for you and your family tree, you secure your Four Walls. Given what you have just been through, the array of possibilities is significant. Perhaps you are among the fortunate for whom there are no issues where these basic needs are concerned. At the other end of the spectrum, you may have been discharged into a world full of confusion and seemingly impossible challenges. Either way, be aware that these things absolutely must be taken care of—and remain taken care of—to protect the integrity of your home so that whatever comes your way, you'll live to fight another day. Survival is the first step toward revival.

Feed your family. That's priority one. Keep them clothed. Keep them healthy. We're talking bare bones—doing only what's absolutely necessary.

Get your family to and from school, work, the grocery, and the pharmacy. Use carpools and public transportation when you can. A paid-for '95 Taurus will get you there just as well as an Escalade with a huge monthly payment.

Pay the rent or your first and second mortgages. Pay your utilities. Run the heat in the winter and some air-conditioning in the summer.

Remember, eating out isn't a necessity. Cable television isn't a utility. One person per car isn't a priority. Five-dollar lattes aren't part of a balanced diet. Use common sense.

When you've taken care of the basics and provided for your household first, you have secured the fortress from which you will conduct your battle with the demons that tried to ruin your life and may have come close to succeeding.

This is a continuing responsibility. You will find that the protection and strengthening of your Four Walls will greatly enhance your ability to gain control—and keep control—of your money.

Don't Go Back into Debt

Debt has not been your friend. Whatever the circumstances were that led you to Bankruptcy, the bottom line is that you owed more money than you were able to pay back on time, and the interest and fees were accumulating and making matters worse.

Do you want to go through that experience again? Well, here's the one-and-only way to make sure that doesn't happen: don't go back into debt.

Before we look at the reasons why it would be better for you to pay cash and buy only what you can afford, let's explore a common myth about the phrase "what you can afford." Most people believe that if they can make the payments, they can afford the purchase. This may be "normal," but it is actually crazy. The very reason you have to make payments is because you can't afford it! You really need to understand that. You don't have the money yourself, so you use someone else's money and pay them for the privilege!

Don't be normal. Be weird. We'll say that over and over. Don't follow the masses that are headed for destruction. Don't fool yourself into believing that four simple words mean something other than what they actually do. "I can afford it," means you have the money. That's it. It doesn't mean, "I can afford to make the payments."

When you pay with cash, you are likely to spend less money! Why? Because spending cash hurts. An MIT study published in Carnegie Mellon magazine found that the pain centers of the brain are activated when you spend cash. This "pain of paying" is much less when plastic is used. On average, card users spend between 12 and 18 percent more.[1] And here's another interesting tidbit: a study in the *Journal of Consumer Research* suggests that people actually spend less when they use crisp new bills than when their money is soiled and crumpled.[2]

When you hand over a Benjamin—a $100 bill with Ben Franklin's picture on it—you really do hate to see him go. Try it. Having that $100 bill in your pocket or purse gives you a sense of security. When you hand it over, you wonder if you are doing the right thing, and you understand that by using it now, you are giving up the ability to use it later for something else that might be more important.

Dave jokes that when you put a $100 bill onto one of those plastic trays that the bill comes in at some restaurants, the tray becomes Uncle Benjamin's coffin. But whether you feel a twinge of regret or not, one thing is certain: The deal is done. Uncle Ben is gone forever!

You are immediately aware of your spending when you use cash. When you hand over the bucks, you know where your money is going. When you wait thirty to forty-five days and make a payment, there's no specific connection between the labor of earning and the joy of acquiring. That's a serious loss.

Think what it would be like to have no debt and no payments at all except maybe your mortgage. What could you save for? What would you dream about doing or having? Write down whatever comes to mind as you think about this. Carry that note with you every day, or put it in a place where you will see it often. Then keep on reading and see how you can make it come true.

Cut Up Your Cards—All of Them

You probably weren't expecting this. Don't make a hasty judgment. Read on and hear us out.

When you hand over a tiny slab of plastic, there really is less pain. There is also more delusion. Even if you are firmly convinced that you will have the money to pay the bill when it comes due, you really don't know for sure.

You have no idea what is going to happen between now and then. You don't know if some gigantic bank is going to tack a premium—in the form of interest and fees—onto the cost of that purchase. So in reality, you don't even know how much you have spent.

Let us clear something up. This isn't aimed only at those of you whose schedule of creditors included the likes of Chase and CitiBank and Bank of America—although one does wonder why card users would want to jump right back into the deep, dark pit from which they had just been rescued. No, it's aimed at everyone. It's aimed at you.

The borrower really is slave to the lender. Don't kid yourself and think otherwise.

Regardless of your politics or philosophy, can anyone actually argue that the country we love isn't on a crash course headed for an economic disaster? Spending money you don't have is simply a bad idea, and the US government has done that to a level that blows the mind. Well, your family system, even if you live alone, is every bit as much subject to the infallible laws of economics as is this country. Pay cash, and the deal is done. Pay with plastic, and the cost is yet to be tallied.

But I need a credit card for hotels and rental cars, you may be thinking. That's just a stinking-thinking fallacy fostered by big banks to keep you as one of their slaves. Dave travels all over the country every week using a debit card, and he manages nicely. So do millions of others, which is why in recent years US debit card transactions have outnumbered credit card transactions, and the gap continues to widen.[3]

You need a credit card to make major purchases, right? Wrong. Stay with us and we'll blow that excuse to smithereens after we deal with saving for emergencies and the dreaded B-word, the budget.

Start Your Emergency Fund

You already know how important it is to save for emergencies in advance. Dave knows it too. His recommended first priority— Baby Step 1—is saving $1,000 for a starter emergency fund.

Why $1,000? Almost anyone can scrape together a thousand dollars in a relatively short time by taking on a second job—or a first job, if that's the situation—or selling some stuff.

Starting small is better than not at all. A $1,000 starter fund will repair the car, fix the broken washer, pay the dentist, and help you weather many of life's storms. Dave calls this paying yourself first.

If you don't already have an emergency fund, think for a moment what life would be like if, when the car needs a minor repair, you simply repaired the car using money you had saved instead of agonizing over what to do and how to do it. Or if, when the furnace decides to be difficult and stops belching heat, you just call the repair people and write a check. Or when your oldest child comes running home with a cut that needs stitches, you go to a clinic without giving your deductible or co-pay another thought. Or when your youngest child needs new shoes, you—wait a minute! Is that an emergency?

This raises an important distinction.

Emergency expenses arise from *unexpected* events. Shoes wearing out—that's to be expected and should be dealt with as a budget item or separately designated savings. This baby emergency fund serves a very important function, and it must be limited to that function—to keep that unexpected event, which is going to happen, from throwing you off track.

You are in charge. You decide what is an emergency. Just use some discretion.

There are two ways to fit an emergency fund into a budget that barely balances. Either increase income or decrease expenses. Income—yes, including that second job referred to above—will be dealt with later. First let's think about decreasing expenses.

Save by Cutting Your Expenses

Be positive. Saying you can't is another way of saying you won't. You really can if you really will. It's being done all the time.

Sell everything that isn't nailed down. Turn that clutter into cash. If you don't need it, sell it! If you haven't touched it in six months, sell it! If you haven't worn it in two years, you're probably sick of it or no longer feel good in it. If you didn't even remember it existed until it turned up, you clearly don't need it. Have a garage sale, or if that's too much hassle, consign it somewhere.

Stop eating out so much. Making your own meals and staying away from your favorite eatery could save you hundreds each month. Add it up! You'll see. Brown-bag your lunch too.

Dave Ramsey still brown-bags with his team every day he's in town. The savings add up quickly. A recent article in *Time* pointed out that "brown-bagging can cut your weekly lunch cost by 80%."[4]

Ditch the cable. Thousands have done it and lived to tell about it. Your family will revolt? Then start with that idea and negotiate down to getting rid of the premium channels and not renting movies on demand. That alone will save the thousand bucks you need to get started.

Break any costly habits. You may not smoke or drink lattes daily, but you do something equally unnecessary on a regular basis, and it's costing you money.

"But we don't make enough money to save!"

Wrong! Saving isn't a matter of how much money you have. It's all about not doing what you know you shouldn't do. You will only cut costs to save money when it becomes an emotional priority. You must focus your emotions instead of letting others do it for you.

Do you really want a better life enough to do whatever it takes?

Then work as hard as you can and live the simplest life possible. Commit to the task. Make it a goal. Sacrifice. Like Dave says, "Live like no one else, so later you can live like no one else."

Save by Increasing Your Short-Term Income

Now, let's look at the other side of the "spend less, earn more" coin.

Begin by scoping out the possibilities at your current workplace. Overtime, weekends, additional assignments—whatever is available to you, take full advantage of it. Keep your eyes peeled for opportunities. Know your skills, and be open to new ways to apply those skills. For that matter, develop new skills. Your employer may even have a program that will pay you and pick up the cost of the training while you learn. Many companies do that because it is smart business.

Suppose you like your job and feel good about staying there, but you aren't eligible for an increase, can't add hours or duties, and don't see any lateral or upward moves on the horizon. Then its time to find that dreaded second job. It may even be time to begin the search for a new first job, but this is about meeting your immediate needs. Improving your career situation will be dealt with later.

Swallow your pride. No work is demeaning. Far from it. Let your extra effort be your badge of honor. You are doing the right thing for the right reasons.

Deliver pizzas. Deliver papers. Rake leaves—rich people hate leaves and will pay someone well to rake them up and haul them off. Mow lawns. Be a Wal-Mart greeter. Be a tool man at Lowe's. Whatever it takes! Some people even get a third job if that's what it takes to change their lives forever!

No one really wants to leave their day job and head to a night shift or stumble out of bed for a crack-of-dawn assignment, but thousands have done it, and many in our offices are doing it right now. You can too. Temporary discomfort is, by definition, temporary. Keep that in mind. A wise man once said that man is able to stand almost anything if he knows it is going to end.

Don't stop at $1,000—fully fund your emergency fund to at least three times your monthly expenses. That will provide a true safety net and let you sleep well.

If you've never experienced the feeling of freedom and peace you get when you are completely out from under the burden of debt and fully prepared for an emergency, you are in for an incredible experience. Whatever small sacrifices you have to make, we assure you it will be worth it.

all about preparing for emergencies so that you ͻwn off track as you get your financial house in order. Now it's time to think about the most important thing you can possibly do to accomplish that daunting task.

Get on a Budget and Stay on It

Budgeting is the process of telling your money where to go before the month begins, instead of wondering where it went after the month is over.

You won't find a more important sentence in this book or a whole lot of others, either.

Budgeting is also an important part of the process of setting goals and establishing priorities. You vote with your money. Everyone does. You identify your values and your priorities by your spending habits for good or ill. What you say may be interesting, but what you do sets your course.

Budgeting can set you free financially and change the spirit of your household. A shared financial plan will eliminate much of the cause of marital conflict. You'll be jointly in control of something that has probably been out of control for a long time. And most of the time people who budget feel like they have gotten a raise, because they are telling their money where to go instead of wondering where it went.

A budget is quite simple, really. It is your plan of matching all your income and all your expenses on paper, on purpose, before the month begins. Note the emphasis on *your*. *You* ultimately control the budget by the choices and designations that you make. If it doesn't work, you will change it.

Here are some budgeting principles to think about:

- If you're married, both spouses must sign off on the budget. The tasks can be divided according to your strengths, but you both must sit down and agree to what's on paper. Listen to and respect each other.

- If you're single, get an accountability partner. Bounce big money decisions off of this trustworthy person. He or she should also have the freedom to confront you firmly but respectfully if you mess up.

- A budget is not a weapon. It should never be used to discipline, chastise, or correct another person, or yourself for that matter.

- There should be no exceptions! Spend every dime on paper. No more "his money" or "her money."

- Be patient. Give yourself three to four months to get the hang of budgeting. It won't be perfect the first time, but don't be discouraged.

- Overfund your groceries category. Most people underfund it and end up with too much month at the end of the food money. It's better to overfund and adjust accordingly once you see how much you realistically spend.

- Again, a budget isn't a straitjacket. It doesn't control you; you control it. You will write it, follow it, and tweak it to make it work.

Once you get into the swing of budgeting, you will be the boss of your bucks. You'll actually experience freedom because you'll be making intelligent, meaningful choices.

Married or single, when you start spending your money on paper on purpose, you'll begin changing your family tree and be on your way to what Dave calls a "Total Money Makeover."

Put Together Your Budget Committee

Does the thought of working with your spouse on a budget make sweat run down your brow? Does it bother you that much to think about turning over all of your power and control to someone else? Guess what. You're not going to have to do that. You're simply transferring that responsibility to a committee of two. Forming your budget committee is intended to accomplish one or both of two purposes. First, it brings to the table the people whose lives are so entwined and interdependent that to make this work, they have to be on board. Second, it adds a new dimension of knowledge and wisdom to the process.

You can spin it in a negative direction if you want to, but pretend you're Doctor Phil for a minute and ask yourself what he would probably ask you: "You've had the power and control up until now. How has that worked for you?"

Husbands and wives have got to be on the same path if they want to end up at the same destination. They must not keep secrets from each other. They must be accountable to each other in a firm but loving way. Singles must find a trusted accountability partner with whom they can have the same kind of "tough love" relationship.

When you surrender half of the power, you relieve yourself of far more than half of the burden. That's good news. Rejoice and be glad that you aren't alone on this path.

Be grateful that there was a judicial system in place to help you find the path to a better future.

Be grateful that there are people who love you and care about you, who will hold you accountable and support you when you need it.

For more specifics on the team concept and the budget committee, you can go to daveramsey.com/tools/budget or to Dave's best-selling books *Financial Peace* and *The Total Money Makeover*.

Master the Budgeting Process

Children do what feels good at the moment, but adults devise a plan and stick with it.

If you want to win with money, you must do what winners do. Giving money a name in your budget also gives it a purpose; that's why it is a key element in financial success. Winners don't wonder where their money went. They tell it where to go and make it go there. Nothing will change until you do.

First, calculate your monthly income from all sources. But don't even think about budgeting with money that *might* come in. Start the process by dealing only with certainty.

If your income is irregular, that presents special challenges. Build your budget with reasonable averages or estimates. Better yet, use a form created for that purpose.

Next, list the expenses that must be paid in the coming month. Gather all of your bills—even the ones you have tried not to think about. Do not hold anything back. You cannot solve a problem you won't face. If you don't have a bill yet, make your best estimate based on past history. Prioritize your expenses by their importance and necessity, beginning with food, clothing, shelter, utilities, and transportation. Remember the Four Walls we mentioned earlier?

Allocate amounts for all your expenses. Overestimate the amount for food at first until you have budgeted enough times to have a good feel for this number. Food is the most likely budget buster. And remember, food includes eating out only when it's absolutely necessary, and even then as little and as reasonable as possible.

When you get to the end of the expenses, you should have a zero balance. Remember, give *every dollar* a name. If you have extra income after allocating for all of your expenses, add more to your saving or giving categories. If you have a negative balance, you'll need to decrease an allocation in one or more categories to bring the bottom line to zero. But be reasonable; you're going to be living off this list.

Forms will make the process much easier. We recommend the ones Dave has on his website: daveramsey.com. Anxious to get started? You can create a sample budget online in sixty seconds at daveramsey.com/tools/budget-lite/.

Here's a final word to the wise. The budget process works when it is embraced fully. Don't go into this half-hearted or pitch in only to avoid criticism or to please your spouse. Make the commitment. Go all in.

Make Major Purchases Without a Credit Card

We said we would get back to this, and here we are.

Credit hasn't been your friend. You really don't want to let that demon back into your life. But life must go on, and there will be times when you need something that costs a fair amount of money.

The key to being able to save—whether for an emergency fund, a child's education, or that major purchase you need to make—is focused emotion and disciplined decision making. You will save for something that is a first priority to you. That has been proven time and time again. And it's not a matter of lip service, either. In fact, what you say is meaningless. You declare your priorities by how you use your money. Everyone does.

Emotions make great slaves, but they are lousy masters. No matter how educated or sophisticated you are, if you are not saving, you are being enslaved by your emotions. Harness those emotions and make them part of your financial plan. Take pride in doing things the common-sense way instead of feeling victimized because you can't keep doing what you've been doing. And don't whine about how hard it is to wait. That's an important behavior change.

Here's a promise. If you will discipline yourself to embrace the simplicity of buying only what you need, spending only what you have, and saving up to pay for major nonemergency purchases, you will truly find financial peace.

What makes a purchase "major"? Is it the dollar amount? Is it a balancing act between the amount and the necessity/desirability? Is it a matter of whether it's a legitimate "need" or simply a "want"? We suggest that both individuals and couples decide on a dollar limit so that the definition of "major" is set in stone. With couples, that establishes the line below which one may make the purchase without the other's advice and consent. That settles a lot of conflict in advance.

Instead of paying with someone else's money, why not make major purchases a part of your budgeting process? Remember, it's your money, and you get to decide where it will go. Consider two possible line items. One would be for anticipated repairs and replacements—a slush fund, so to speak—such as a new roof, new tires for the car, and so forth. The other line item would be for specific purchases that you and your spouse or accountability partner agree on. You begin by investigating the choices, selecting the one you want, and adding up the cost. You then determine how much you can budget for that purpose on a monthly basis, and start allocating it. To know when you will actually be able to buy whatever it is, just divide that monthly amount into the total cost. You'll find excitement will build as the allocated fund accumulates, and the purchase will be more fun than ever!

Saving until you can afford it—what a novel concept! Delayed gratification needs to become a way of life. Children act on impulse. Mature adults are willing to postpone the reward until it has been earned.

Changing your behavior requires more than a new attitude. It requires action! Cut all credit cards. Borrow no more. Save for purchases. You're now debt-free—stay that way!

Decide If Your Need Is Really a Want

As part of defining a major purchase, you have to decide if something is really a need or something you just want. Learning to be honest and realistic about needs versus wants is a crucial behavior change. Greed can certainly tip those scales. Don't let it.

Advertisers want you to see your wants as needs, and they will use your emotions to enslave you. They'll do so with skill born of years of experimentation. As a result, one of the most important challenges you will face is determining—make that *admitting*—that a particular item you are considering purchasing is a want rather than a real need.

In today's "normal" family, wants are justified under some twisted application of entitlement. So you've got to be weird and deal honestly with the difference. And this is true for every one of your dependents, be they family members or otherwise. It won't do for one person to live with integrity while those nearby keep doing the same things over and over, expecting a different result. That's the definition of insanity.

This "need versus want" test is one you will face often. Is the purchase really necessary? That's always an issue. If it's not, do you have the strength to resist? When temptation rears its ugly head, the word *no*, standing alone without the need for justification, will work wonders. Try it.

While we are on the matter of words, consider this: for the rest of your life, *ought* must be replaced by *no*. There isn't anything you *ought* to have if you can't afford to pay for it.

If it's definitely a need, then you move on to the next step, which is to put the item in your budget.

Financial peace is possible no matter how old you are, how big a hole you've dug, or how far down the wrong path you've gone. If you're sick and tired of being sick and tired and are willing to do whatever it takes, you can—and will—find peace.

Once you've checked everything off the to-do list, move on to these next steps, and envision yourself that much closer to living like no one else!

Next Steps

Stay Focused During Tough Times

Economic recovery is painfully slow, but remember, when unemployment is at 8 percent, that means 92 percent of American workers have jobs!

Is that an insincere irony? No. It simply illustrates an important point. There are many things you cannot do—change the economy, create jobs, reopen the plant—so you must identify what you can change and work to change it. If you are part of that unfortunate 8 percent, consider this condition temporary—never think of it as permanent. You think mind-set doesn't matter? Think again.

Don't let "the economy" become your destiny. People win in every economy. Great companies and great careers have been born in tough times.

Fear and hopelessness lead to paralysis. You can either give in to paralysis or go about life in fiscally responsible ways, as normally as possible.

Focus on your skills and interests. How can you leverage your passions into something you enjoy and get paid to do? Believe this is possible, because it is.

If you are unemployed, look for work while looking for "that" job. A job is a point on a career path leading upward. Work is a means to an end, tolerable because it's temporary. Being occupied will do wonders for your spirits. Deliver papers or pizzas, bag groceries, blow leaves—whatever you can find. Take on every task as a volunteer, not as a victim. "Be the job big or small, do it well or not at all."

Take one day at a time. Be thankful that you are alive, healthy, and on your way back to where you want to be. The rest of your life lies in front of you. Take back your power. Decide what you want, and then go get it.

Somewhere in America the next Bill Gates is tinkering with a computer and inching toward an amazing discovery. The next Mary Kay is coming up with a product women will crawl over each other to buy. The next Hobby Lobby is doing a booming business in someone's garage.

America is still the land of opportunity. Don't miss that. You are much more in charge of your destiny than you know.

Find the Work That Fits You Best

What are you going to do with the rest of your working life? Maybe you made bad decisions and became a slave to lenders. Or maybe you got caught in circumstances beyond your control. In any case, let's use that experience to change the future. Those who do not learn from the past are doomed to repeat it.

The seven dwarfs whistled while they worked. Do you? Some lucky people really hop out of bed energized and head for a place where work has meaning. Are you one of those? Maybe you feel trapped in a job you struggle to endure until the weekend comes. As Dave often says, "Thank God it's Friday—oh God, it's Monday" is a really awful way to live.

What about your income? Do you worry that you'll repeat a past filled with pinched pennies and juggled budgets? You aren't alone. Most debtors aren't discharged onto a gilded path. Have faith in yourself. Listen to your own inner voice. From the very same spot you can either walk down a dead-end road or climb an upward path. The choice is yours.

Dave speaks from experience when he declares that money is ultimately an empty goal. His advice? "Find something you love doing so much that on the tough days you have a reason to fight on." Can you imagine what it would be like to do something you love every day and get paid for it?

I could've done that by now if I'd really wanted to, you might be thinking. Really? In his best-selling book, *Quitter*, Jon Acuff says that's how we shift the blame for failing to take that first step toward our dream job. We convince ourselves that it's really too late. But it's never too late. [5]

What would you do if money didn't matter? The answer will be the starting point on your track from day job to dream job. Read *Quitter*. It will help you get "wired up and fired up" and ready to make changes for the better.

Jon's newest book, *Start*, is filled with inspiration to help you get unstuck by punching fear in the face, escaping average, and doing work that matters.

Money does matter, of course. Dave urges you to put work clothes on your dream. In his best-seller *EntreLeadership* he shows you how to turn a vision into a goal and how to reach that goal through specific, practical action steps.

You may think you are stuck where you are for one reason or another, but you aren't. Get over that. Nobody's stuck. We're all where we are because we choose to stay there.

Change begins with a promise and a decision. The promise is to make your life better for yourself and those you love. The decision is to quit talking about it and get started doing it.

Don't put it off. Read those two books. They have changed many lives. Then take charge and embrace the change that's ahead for you. You won't regret it.

Quit Worshipping at the Altar of FICO

Dave Ramsey hates debt, and he seriously wonders why anyone would want to rebuild a FICO score to begin with. This is playing with snakes and hoping you don't get bitten. We agree with him.

You can start out resolved to do better, but you can't stop being human. A rebuilt credit score could easily lead to borrowing money—a little at first, perhaps—and the next thing you know you're paying interest and piling up debt again after going through a gut-wrenching, marriage-twisting experience that resulted from being in debt in the first place. This is not a pretty picture.

FICO is one of the great marketing scams in American history. In the FICO score, debt history counts 35 percent, current debt 30 percent, length of time in debt 15 percent, and type of debt and new debt 10 percent each. FICO doesn't take into account the individual's employment situation, past or current income, debt-to-income ratio, cash on hand, or net worth.

Ignoring those important elements while allegedly assessing a person's ability to pay makes no sense at all. It's idiotic. Yet FICO somehow convinced the financial world that being employed and having savings or a net worth in the millions had nothing to do with credit worthiness.

As a discharged debtor who has been through the mill and gone through the system, you'll find that lenders will make it remarkably easy for you if you let them. They know you were willing to spend money you didn't have the first time around, and they're betting you'll do it again. They also know that you won't be able to go bankrupt for years. "You sign, you're mine" is their mantra.

Dave hopes you will focus instead on building wealth and changing your family tree. For twenty-five years he has been teaching people how to do that through his program *Financial Peace University*, touching the lives of more than 1.5 million families in the process.

Dave would remind you that you have climbed a very steep hill—one tough task indeed—but you faced it and did it. You can either stay on top or head back downhill to FICO land and risk crashing again. Which one will bring you peace?

Monitor All Three of Your Credit Reports

Some 79 percent of all credit reports contain errors.[6] Even though you shouldn't make financial decisions based on it, FICO is still a reality. Your FICO score needs at least to present an accurate picture.

Three major companies—Equifax, Experian, and TransUnion—issue credit reports in essentially the same format, and your FICO score is based on all three reports. You can get one free copy of each company's report once a year at annualcreditreport.com. Your credit reports will have four major sections: Identifying Information, Credit History, Public Records, and Inquiries.

The Identifying Information section lists your name, address, social security number, date of birth, and other personal information.

The Credit History section shows open accounts, late payments, balances, credit limits, and payment history. Make sure all of the information is correct.

The Public Records section lists tax liens, lawsuits, and judgments. You'd like for it to be blank, but it's too late for that, so make sure it's accurate.

The Inquiries section will list everyone who has asked to see your credit report—soft inquiries when companies want to check on you or send you something, and hard inquiries when you fill out a credit application.

If you find an error, send a letter demanding a correction via certified mail, deliver to addressee only, return receipt requested. State the facts. Explain what is wrong and why. If the responsible credit bureau hasn't resolved the matter after thirty days, they have to remove the item no matter what they have found out.

Make sure to check about six months after your discharge to see if all of the credit accounts discharged in bankruptcy are accurately listed as discharged.

Having said all that, we can recommend a service that will do all of the clean-up work for you.

For years, bankruptcy attorney Raef J. Granger advised his clients to make sure the three credit bureaus knew about their discharge. Most thought the bankruptcy process did that automatically and were disappointed to learn that wasn't the case.

To solve this problem he founded RocketDog Reports, a company specializing in post-bankruptcy updating and refreshing. Check them out at RocketDogReports.com. They do charge a small fee for their services.

Buy the Right Kinds of Insurance

There are several kinds of insurance that ought to be considered as part of a sound financial plan at any economic level. This is true because there are different kinds of unavoidable risks in life. An accident at home can result in personal liability. Accidents and illnesses are inevitable. Identity theft is often devastating. Insurance can be a godsend.

Auto liability is universally required. Deciding on collision coverage may come down to a decision regarding the value of the car.

Term life insurance in an amount ten times annual income will meet most families' needs. Life insurance is important for the non-breadwinner too. Do not discount the value of a spouse's contribution or the cost of replacing their services.

Identity theft insurance is an absolute must. It is relatively inexpensive, covers your loss, and provides someone to do the legwork and paperwork.

Buy homeowner's coverage and personal liability. The need for flood insurance in certain areas has been dramatized recently, although it may be hard to get. If you rent, buy renter's insurance and personal liability. Your landlord may insure the building, but your belongings are not covered. List your valuables and heirlooms on a personal property rider. Most homeowner's policies have strict exclusions for certain kinds of unlisted valuables. It is well worth the money.

Health insurance is part of a solid financial plan. If you've been to the doctor or stayed in a hospital, you know that. Medical expenses are one of the top causes of bankruptcy. Don't think you can make it without health insurance. When you play with fire, you risk getting badly burned.

According to *USA Today*, 24 percent of people working after retirement age are doing so because they need health coverage.[7] In the near future, work may not guarantee health benefits because the cost to employers has skyrocketed. With the changes that we know about and the changes we don't yet know or understand, it is risky to offer advice in this area. But here are some suggestions:

If you end up having to get health insurance on your own, use an agent who has the heart of a teacher and can explain things in layman's terms, and never buy anything you do not understand.

Try to take on as much of a deductible as you can in order to get the lowest premiums available. One good option is the Health Savings Account (HSA). A family can save a designated amount tax free to use toward their health insurance deductible. This means you can save by carrying a high-deductible HSA insurance policy.

There is no magic pill for paying medical bills, but hospitals and doctors are frequently willing to work out terms for payment. If you get in a mess with medical bills, go to the hospital or doctor's business office—hat in hand—and show them your budget. That will let them know what you can do and can't do.

At age sixty or beyond, seriously consider long-term care insurance. The cost of extended care can destroy a nest egg in a heartbeat.

For all insurance, use an independent agent who works with many insurance companies. A top-flight agent can find the policy that fits your needs best.

Protect Your Family Against Identity Theft

The Identity Theft Resource Center reported that 23 million Americans had their Social Security number, driver's license number, medical records, or financial accounts exposed in 2011.[8] Unfortunately, your bankruptcy created one more record to be hacked.

Bank statements, credit card applications, checks—all are there for the taking in your trash, mail, and wallet or purse. Thieves get your debit card numbers from a corporate database. They'll watch your fingers while you type your PIN at an ATM or pick it up just from the sound of it being typed.

They can be right behind you, and you'll never even know it. And once they have this information, they can wreck your good name. Before you know what has happened, they can commit several crimes and create quite a mess.

Here are some serious red flags to watch out for:

- Checks disappearing from your checkbook

- Credit reports showing accounts you don't recognize

- Bills or collection calls about accounts you did not open

- Late-arriving bank and billing statements

- Statements that appear to have been tampered with

- Unauthorized charges on any of your accounts

If you think you've been a victim, file a police report immediately. Check your credit report and card statements. Cancel any suspicious accounts. If your purse or wallet is stolen, cancel all cards and get replacements.

Put a stop-payment order on all lost or stolen cards. Contact one of the three main credit-reporting companies—Experian, Equifax, and TransUnion—to put a fraud alert on your credit report. That company will alert the other two.

Be proactive. Be extra careful about how and where you carry cards and checks, where you keep important papers, how much personal information you give out and to whom, and be extra alert for those warning signs.

Buy identity theft insurance. It's remarkably inexpensive, and an absolute must in this day and age. If you become a victim, not only are you financially protected against loss, but even more importantly they'll assign someone to your case to do all of the legwork and paper work. That alone is worth way more than the premium.

Set Goals and Plan Your Better Life

Dare to dream of a better future. Go for it. There's absolutely nothing wrong with having a dream, unless that's as far as you get. Unfortunately, some people spend their lives massaging their dream and draining their emotions until they develop a victim mentality because their dream doesn't come true.

Once you believe in your dream, it's time to take action and turn that dream into a goal. A goal is a dream dressed in work clothes.

Are you a goal setter? Do you typically set goals at the first of the year or at some other time that is important to you? If not, why not?

Goals give you a starting point and a destination. Setting them is the easiest way to give meaningful direction to your life, which releases you to effectively use your talents.

So what do you want to accomplish and become from this point on? Yes, we're talking about "now," before you have even finished this book!

Tomorrow doesn't have to be like yesterday, and this year doesn't have to be like previous years. You can set goals and keep them. You can decide now how you want your future to be.

What is your goal for tomorrow? What do you want to see in your mind's eye when you put your head on your pillow and look back over the day?

Don't just dream about how you wish things would be. Develop a plan and make it happen!

You start the goal-setting process with a clean sheet of paper and a pen. Yes, you can use a computer, but something amazing happens when you take the time to write down your goals on a piece of paper and carry it with you wherever you go as a constant reminder.

Goals that will really work for you must be:

- Specific
- Measurable
- Yours
- Time-sensitive
- Written

Identify the action steps. The goal is your destination. The action steps are your plan for getting there. That's how the impossible becomes manageable.

Be realistic. Think about what you believe you can accomplish toward reaching your goal during a specific time, such as a calendar year. Make action steps measurable so you can track your progress. Don't rush things. Give each step the time and attention it needs.

Anything worth doing requires discipline. Yet it's important not to get discouraged if your goal isn't accomplished in the exact way and in the precise time frame as you originally planned. Some flexibility is needed. As long as you are focused on the goal and are taking proactive steps toward achieving it, you're an achiever, and you're on your way to doing great things.

Your dream will become a reality only if you take steps toward it. Here are some examples of goals you might start with:

- (If you want to start exercising) Walk or jog thirty minutes, three times a week.
- (If you want to buy a nicer car) Save $100 per month in a car fund.
- (If you want to spend more time with your family) Dedicate one or two nights a week to sit all together at the table for dinner and talk about your day.

Don't set your goal so high that you have no chance to hit the mark. Don't make it so big that the weight of it will eventually immobilize you. Begin with simple goals that you have a high chance of reaching, because small successes inevitably lead to larger ones.

Change Your Behavior

Personal finance really is 20 percent head knowledge and 80 percent behavior. That's what Dave has preached to millions of people for a quarter of a century, and he has yet to be proven wrong.

Finding financial peace isn't just a matter of what you know, even though education is important. The solution goes beyond book learning. Way beyond. Let's face it. If knowledge really were all it took, you wouldn't be emerging from bankruptcy. You would have already solved this problem.

So how do you keep from slipping back into your old, destructive ways? The solution is to change your behavior by replacing those old patterns with new ones that work, patterns that will lead you and your family to genuine financial peace.

There's no blame to be assigned here. Like everyone else, you are the product of the sum total of your life's experiences. You did what you thought was best, which is what most Americans do. But it didn't work then, and the same behavior won't work now. Knowing that, if you don't change, the fault will be yours.

Changing your behavior is a multi-level challenge. You must learn to be intentional and not reactive. Impulses will still happen—you'll still see something you feel like you simply *must have*. Your priorities have to change. Self-discipline isn't easy. Delayed gratification must become a way of life.

Most of all, you must face the truth about entitlement. You aren't entitled to anything. No one—including life itself—owes you anything.

Start by being honest with your most dangerous enemy, the man or woman who stares back at you in your mirror. Admit it because it's true—if you keep on doing what you have been doing, you will keep on getting what you have been getting.

For example, let's say credit card debt is what pushed you over the edge. That would be obvious to outsiders like your lawyer and the court, but suppose you don't admit it to yourself. The likelihood that you will walk right back into the credit card trap would be dangerously high.

You simply must come out of the dark and begin living in the light. There can't be any more secrecy around even the smallest financial decision. Deception will never be appropriate. In the beginning you must make every financial decision out in the open, accessible to someone you can trust.

What you will find, to your delight, is that honesty is every bit as habit-forming as secrecy, and it never leaves a bad feeling in your heart or a bad taste in your mouth.

Your Place in the Real World

Will filing bankruptcy haunt you, label you, and keep you from improving yourself? The answer is up to you. It will do all of those if you let it. But the good news is that you do not have to let it!

As we reminded you at the outset, the bankruptcy laws were created to give people a second chance, a fresh start. That's good news. Your attitude toward your fresh start is a matter of choice, not chance. It will be whatever you make it through hard work and careful choices.

If you were one of those debtors who was blindsided by the expenses of an illness, accident, or catastrophe, we are sincerely sorry.

If you did stupid things with money, welcome to the club. In America, that's normal. You may not deserve a pat on the back, but you also don't need to hang your head in shame or go around with a scarlet "B" sewn on your shirt.

Let's face it: public perception about bankruptcy runs the gamut from open hostility to guarded acceptance. Nobody is in love with the idea, and some people even think the whole system is unfairly and intentionally designed to help people get out of their debt by shifting the burden to their creditors. That's not a pleasant attitude, nor one that offers much slack, but honestly, that's part of what you are facing.

It isn't important what others think, but what you think makes all the difference in the world. What really matters is where you are right now and what you are going to do from now on.

Let's begin by eliminating some false targets you might be tempted to aim at instead of accepting appropriate personal responsibility for what you have been through.

It isn't discriminatory for prospective employers, lenders, or people with whom you might contract to ask if you have ever filed for bankruptcy. It isn't prohibited by any law or court decision. It's not an invasion of privacy, either. It's a legitimate issue of importance. It's not as if it were a big secret. Court records are public except in extraordinary cases, which yours is probably not. You should expect the question of bankruptcy to come up when it is relevant, such as when applying for work, especially in positions dealing with finances.

There isn't a good way to spin what you have been through, but really, a "spin" might not be necessary. People file for bankruptcy for all sorts of legitimate reasons—unpredicted emergencies, job loss, etc. And even if yours was based solely on personal failure, facts are facts. You are better off demonstrating change than struggling to avoid reality. You certainly don't want to begin any important relationships with deceptions or half-truths.

You should handle any legitimate, appropriate questions about your bankruptcy by answering honestly. Spill your guts? Of course not! Base your revelations on your best "need to know" judgment given the circumstances. You can add more to an admission, but you can't retract what you have already made public.

Note our use of the words "legitimate and appropriate." That phrase covers a very small group, which doesn't include the idly curious or the chronic gossipers. Your situation isn't cocktail party banter or dinner table conversation. Use "need to know" as your yardstick to decide who you should tell, as well as how much you should tell. Whatever you choose to reveal, tell the truth. An honest person never has to worry about remembering what was said.

Prepare responses to possible questions before they are asked, and when you expect questions to be raised, show integrity by volunteering appropriate information. Don't be apologetic, but also don't be arrogant. Try not to have a chip on your shoulder. Be open, honest, and clear in your disclosure, and do it with appropriate humility.

Then there is the sensitive matter of close family—especially your children—and certain intimate friends. These are a special class needing special rules.

Respect your family's privacy even more than your own. Some or all of your immediate family members were probably taken on this trip against their will. Don't make it any harder on them than it absolutely has to be.

Most of all, don't try to pretend that nothing has happened. Denial is a painful burden. And don't feel self-conscious or have even a small pity-party. People who really love you and care about you aren't looking to judge you; they want to help you. Welcome that help.

Learn everything you possibly can about how to handle money responsibly. Choose your "teachers" carefully—select only those with proven track records. Using your new knowledge, change your behavior where money is concerned. That is really how you can change your family tree.

Dave Ramsey has paid stupid tax with lots of zeros. Twenty-five years ago he came out of personal bankruptcy and began to put his life on track. Instead of normal, he chose weird. He decided to never again owe any money to anyone. You, too, must become weird and proud of it. You must clean house, dump the habits and attitudes that didn't work, and replace them with ones that will take you where you want to go.

Develop a Healthy Level of Disgust

What kind of behavior caused you to end up in bankruptcy court? Many filings are caused by life itself—natural disasters, tragic accidents, serious illnesses, economic downturns, layoffs, and firings—and they are not what this chapter is about. But reckless spending and the irresponsible use of credit cause an alarming number of bankruptcy cases, and make even more cases much worse than they might have been had the people involved not misbehaved with their money.

Millions of Americans are addicted to spending. Thousands of them call *The Dave Ramsey Show* every year looking for a way out of that self-created dilemma. More often than not, they've bought stuff they didn't need with money they didn't have to impress people they don't like and sometimes don't even know.

Some people can be classified as "shopaholics." These are the really compulsive spenders. But most people who spend their way into trouble are simply reckless and immature. They've grown up without ever being told no, and they've failed to shed that mentality as time wore on. As adults, they don't know how to tell themselves no.

Reckless spending can have a huge impact on a marriage, especially when neither party believes it is reckless in the first place. That's a major problem in our society.

Normal people want things and charge them to some credit account when they don't have the money to pay for them and don't know where that money will come from when the debt is due. The Smiths see the Joneses accumulating shiny, fancy stuff. They get jealous, begin to feel entitled, then march out and buy something even shinier, fancier, and more unnecessary! Welcome to 21st-century America!

When the bill comes due and the money isn't there, or when other more important things have to wait because these bills have to be paid, each party blames the other for their joint bad judgment. Disagreement becomes friction. Tension escalates. Trouble is no longer just brewing—it has fully brewed and spilled over.

According to some experts, financial stress is the number-one cause of divorce. That may not seem obvious at first, but think about it. When you add serious financial problems to a situation where communication barely exists and control is the order of the day, where is that likely to lead? Will there be violence? Infidelity? Abandonment? Those might be among the listed causes when such fractured relationships finally explode, but what started it all is how they dealt with their money.

Here's what Dave told a caller who had described his reckless spending: "Number one: You've got to really believe you have a problem. Sometimes, you need a healthy level of disgust with yourself to make a change. Then you've got to realize that the next spending run you make is going to cost you the marriage. If you get that into your head, then you will change."

Adults devise a plan and follow it; children do what feels good. If you have recognized your spending problem, then you have taken the first step. Now it's time to follow through.

Break Entitlement's Grip

Before getting into the meat of this topic, we want you to try a little exercise we've come up with just for you. Well, for you and millions of others. This involves your face, so first time around you might want to do this when you are by yourself.

Begin by smiling slightly and parting your lips and teeth—not much, just a little. Then place your tongue against the roof of your mouth right where the roof of your mouth meets your front teeth. Don't worry about being too precise. Just relax and try this until you are comfortable doing it.

Now, hum. Any old note will do. Got that down? Here comes the last part. While humming, pull your tongue down and back, away from its front-of-the-mouth position, and quickly form a tight circle with your lips.

If you did it right, you just said, "No."

Now that you have mastered that word, start using it. Begin by telling yourself, "No, you aren't entitled to anything," or "No, they don't owe it to you," or that really serious one, "No, it wasn't their fault; it was your fault."

The point? The world doesn't owe you a living, or anything else, for that matter. You may sometimes feel put upon and entitled, but hear this clearly: you're not. And if you let such thoughts take up residence, you are headed for big trouble. You simply must tell yourself no.

Your spouse doesn't owe you anything. Neither do your kids, your parents, or any family members. The same is true for the company you work for and the people you work with. Like it or not, you are not entitled to any special treatment, favors, or things.

The feeling of entitlement is a product of unresolved anger at someone or something that you believe has been unfair to you and held you back. Unresolved anger festers into resentment. Instead of resolving it in a healthy way, you convince yourself that "their" action justifies your doing something that you ordinarily would not do. To bring the scales of human justice to an even position, you buy something you neither need nor can afford, or go a step further and do something that you never would have done had you been thinking straight.

Eventually you may cross a moral or ethical line—a small one, at first—to get something you feel entitled to. Once the self-destructive cycle is in place, justification becomes easier, and the excitement of getting away with something becomes hypnotic and enticing.

Deception becomes a way of life as you hide your behavior from those you love, as well as those who have allegedly done you wrong. Can you see where this leads? Yielding to a feeling of entitlement can destroy your marriage, your relationships, your job—everything you hold dear.

So what do you do to avoid such a pattern?

Turn inward and identify the feelings that signal the onset of entitlement. That won't be hard at all once you understand what is happening to you.

Turn those feelings to your advantage by letting them be warning signals that announce the approach of trouble with a capital T. Armed with a new awareness and alerted by this new way of looking at things, you can then stop the feelings in their tracks and expose them as lies.

So you've marked off your to-do list and addressed the next steps. Now we'll discuss a few more areas you'll want to cover to ensure your financial future is a peaceful one.

Advice for Moving Forward

Don't Rebuild Your Credit

We know that the myth of FICO is so solidly woven into the financial fabric of our community that some of you—perhaps many—will want to "rebuild" anyway, in spite of what we say about it. In the interest of steering you away from some of the really bad ideas you will learn about from even a casual search of the web, we offer some suggestions.

Surround yourself with positive people who understand what you are trying to do and who will help you do it. Get on a budget and get control of your money. Include your spouse and kids in this quest. Study carefully how you got into trouble so you can avoid repeating it.

Change your beliefs and your behavior completely. Not just you, but the whole family. Not partially, but completely. Everything you did that contributed to your financial mess needs to be changed. That's a tall order, but it can be done.

Expect to be inundated with offers of credit, and take pleasure in trashing them. Just for kicks, keep a running tally of how much credit you are offered. That number alone ought to wake you up as to what they are trying to get you to do.

From the day you commit to rebuilding your credit, your financial record must be spotless. Utility bills, insurance payments, and doctors' bills—all must be paid on time. Other ordinary obligations must be met according to their terms. But borrow money on a credit card just so you can turn around and pay it back?

Some so-called experts recommend that. Dave does not. In a perfect world, with perfect people, that might work. But you'd be placing yourself at risk of making yet another bad decision, the same kind that brought so much pain and grief before.

Use a debit card, which is a smarter and better way to go. Smartest of all would be to sign up for *Financial Peace University* and learn how to live on a cash basis and build real wealth!

Dave also has programs for kids, teenagers, and college students. Best-selling books, specialized programs, online opportunities—there's a little something for everyone. Check out daveramsey.com and find out what is available.

Consider Alternative Credit Reporting

What if there is a better way than FICO? You agree in principle with Dave and don't want to take on new debt after your discharge. You have managed to avoid doing that, thanks to a good job and some welcome new behaviors. You're thinking about owning a home again, and you've even saved up for a down payment.

"Sorry," says FICO. Your income, the bills you've been paying on time for months or years, your savings, the assets you've accumulated—they don't count. Your lingering low credit score will stop you in your tracks. What if there was a satisfactory alternative to, and even a better way than, FICO? Well, maybe there is.

We're talking about eCredable, a credit-worthiness calculator that looks at how well and how consistently you pay your bills on time. That's essentially what the mortgage companies, landlords, and other legitimate lenders want to know, isn't it? The big issue with them is whether or not you are likely to pay them back on time.

The folks at eCredable look at how often and consistently you pay your rent, insurance, cell phone bill, etc. They plug your info into a formula and give you a report showing your "grade" on paying things back using an F to A scale. Many lenders and landlords have started accepting this because it tells them what they want to know the most. We believe its use will increase with time.

You can learn a lot more by going to eCredable.com/DRDE.

Is this an endorsement? No. It's just important information about a service we know about which, for now, looks like something that will help a lot of people who want to rent, get a mortgage, or enter into any other transaction where the lenders still worship blindly at the feet of the almighty FICO. It's not the only possibility—it's just one we know about. And we know it's a better option than the brain-dead application of the stupid FICO formula.

Become a Fast-Moving Target

Let's face it. You're a target. Every predatory lender out there knows your history. They know about your bankruptcy. They know what got you where you are. They are just lying in wait for you to come their way.

You're going to be tempted by a lot of "easy credit" offers. You're probably already getting them in the mail every day, sometimes more than one, and a lot of them at zero percent interest. On paper they will really look good. The most poisonous snakes are beautiful from a safe distance.

Blood suckers will keep on coming out of the woods, their excitement palpable, and their words dripping with false sincerity. They'll come offering just what you need the least right now—more credit! But when that word is uttered, think debt! That's what credit is—more debt—and the more honest you are with yourself about that, the more you will work to avoid it.

Don't even think about it!

Even if you're able to resist the most ludicrous of these siren calls, you may be tempted to use "rebuilding your credit" as an excuse to jump back into that pit. But if you take off those rose-colored glasses and admit that debt is what got you in trouble in the first place, you're far less likely to try to take that path again.

It's just a piece of plastic, you'll tell yourself. And you've changed! You've learned your lesson! From now on you'll buy only what you have to have and absolutely pay off the bill every month.

The road to poverty is paved with those kinds of good intentions. You may honestly and sincerely believe whatever you tell yourself, but think for a minute. Why do you suppose you're getting those offers?

These people are predators! They know what you've been through, but they are coming after you anyway! They think they can make even more money off of you, knowing that you can't go back to court for relief any time soon. Predatory lenders aren't trying to make your life better. Don't give them a single dime of your hard-earned money.

Think back to what it was like right before you filed bankruptcy. Remember the pain, the anxiety, the embarrassment, the endless calls and letters, the harassment, and the ungodly amount you were paying them in interest, fees, and whatever other charges they could think of.

Don't play with fire! You've already been burned once!

You Can Buy a Home In Spite of Bankruptcy

We have good news: the American Dream is not out of reach for you. But don't even think about such a purchase until your emergency fund is fully funded with an amount that equals three to six months of your household expenses. You don't want your dream home to turn into another nightmare.

As in the case of renting, do the math. Be detailed. Be realistic. Be absolutely certain you can afford to buy a home. And never buy more house than you can afford. You can move up later when your situation improves.

Again, as is the case with renting, don't go see places that are out of range for you. Whatever house you look at, you'll be greeted by an utterly charming man or woman who will claim to have all kinds of tricks up their sleeve to help you "afford" that house. But remember, that person's income depends on their ability to get you to sign on the line. That's their main goal.

So what is your range of affordability? You must be able to put down a minimum of 15 to 20 percent, using your own money and not drawing down existing allocated savings. You should finance for no more than fifteen years at a fixed rate, with the whole monthly payment never exceeding 25 percent of your take-home pay.

If you can meet those parameters, don't waste time applying for financing with a brain-dead lender that considers your FICO credit score the most important factor—maybe even the only factor. You'll be turned down, and that will make your record look even worse.

Find a lender that does individual underwriting, one that considers things that really matter, such as income, assets, and character. Lenders will tell you their criteria if you just ask.

Be prepared to tell an honest story, but one that emphasizes the triumph instead of the tragedy. Document all experiences that demonstrate your reliability, such as your longevity at work, your record of paying rent on time, your on-time history with other monthly expenses such as utilities, cable, etc. Consider a rent-to-buy situation. In a down market, a long-suffering seller may be open to this possibility, so don't hesitate to bring it up.

Emergency funds, college savings, and retirement accounts are strictly off-limits as a down payment. You will be tempted. After all, that money is just sitting there. But this is time for an adult attitude. Remember, children do what feels good; adults have a plan and stick to it.

Never borrow under the table from friends or family. The borrower is the slave of the lender. They may want to help. They may even say you don't have to pay it back until sometime in the future. Don't do it. Don't ask them to co-sign your note, either. That's no better for them than it is for you.

Can you accept a gift from a friend or loved one? Absolutely, as long as you know for sure that there are no strings attached.

On the Other Hand, Consider Renting

You're not in a position to buy, so renting offers the only viable option. But your FICO score has been trashed big time.

You already know that most apartment complexes aren't going to want to rent to you based on that alone. Good or bad, right or wrong—none of that matters. That's how thoroughly FICO has poisoned the water.

Is your situation hopeless? Absolutely not. Are there things you can do to help your cause? Yes, there are. And the key is to thoroughly prepare every aspect of your case in advance. Don't just hop in the car and drive from place to place hoping you'll get lucky. That would be a huge waste of time.

First and foremost, you should calculate exactly how much rent you can afford based on your circumstances. This should not exceed 25 percent of your take-home pay. Be smart. Don't put yourself in harm's way by looking too closely at places that will cost more than you ought to spend.

Be aware of what's going on in your market. Look for news reports about struggling developments that are desperate for tenants. There are lots of them.

Watch for names of individual owners who need tenants. Look on the bulletin board at church, the library, or a community center. Drive around and look for signs.

Document your case. Use common sense. Establish a record of meeting obligations on time, whatever they are (electric bill, water bill, phone bill, etc.). Get recommendations from people with whom you've been reliable.

Sell yourself. Tell potential landlords what you've been through. Give them every reason you can come up with why you are the tenant they've been hoping for all along. Remember, you're creating your own "renting résumé."

When it's time to sign a lease, pay a good real estate lawyer to read over it, and don't sign it until you understand every obligation you're taking on.

Once you have moved in, pay your rent on time, every month—no exceptions, no excuses. You will create a valuable, positive reference for the future by being super reliable and responsible in spite of your bankruptcy.

The Reaffirmed Mortgage Now Upside Down

Okay, you've been discharged. You reaffirmed your home—it was a good idea at the time—but thanks to the economy, you're now upside-down. There's no way you can make the payments. Should you walk away?

Once again, you can take some comfort in knowing that you're not alone. According to one reliable survey, 27 percent of unfortunate homeowners are in that same position.[9]

There's no right way to do the wrong thing. Walking away from a mortgage is an unwise and inappropriate solution to a serious problem.

The so-called experts who actually advise people to walk away are saying what people want to hear so they can sell whatever they are selling. Truth is, you can't avoid paying the difference between what you owe the bank and what the house brings. It may take longer, but banks still go after their money, adding interest, expenses, and eye-popping legal fees.

If you were shopping for a home right now, this would be a great time to buy. If it's a good time to buy, it's a good time to keep what you have. Walking away in a down market is selling your investment at the bottom.

You signed a contract. You're legally and morally obligated. If you can't handle the payment and keep food on the table, talk with the bank about a short sale. Lay the facts on the table.

Banks have no interest in beating a dead horse, and they most certainly don't want to own a lot of real estate. In fact, Federal Regulations keep them from doing so. You may be surprised at what kind of arrangement you can make if you put some effort into it.

Home values may recover in your area. In some places the upward trend has already started. If you stick it out and stay in your home, you'll be even in five years based on a conservative 5-percent rate of appreciation. In less than twenty years your home will have doubled in value.

If you jump off the roller coaster at the bottom of the loop, not only will you be hurt, but you'll miss the ride back up too.

The Home You Can No Longer Afford

Sometimes you just can't make the numbers work no matter how you juggle the figures. Sometimes you're going to have to surrender your home.

Surrendering your home does not relieve the lender of having to go through proper legal channels to sell the property. You will have some breathing room. How much time will you have before you have to move your family out? We get asked that often. People panic and think they're going to be kicked out onto the street with their things piled on the sidewalk. But the foreclosure process is always regulated by statute, and the statute contains fixed time periods the lender must follow.

You will be notified by certified mail to your last known address. We know of no jurisdiction where this does not happen.

Be sure the lender always knows where you are, or they will use the address of the property. If you are no longer there, they do not have to try to find you.

The foreclosure notice must contain a full legal description of the property and the exact date, time, and location of the sale.

You may be allowed to stay at a reduced rent in exchange for keeping the place up and having it look nice to show to prospective buyers. Ask about that. If you make arrangements to stay and pay rent, pay on time every month.

Take as good care of the property as you can afford. Don't get angry and trash it. This is an important part of reestablishing yourself as a reliable, fiscally responsible person of integrity.

If you come across an acceptable alternative in a short time, you do not have to stay until the sale takes place unless your mortgage states otherwise. Notify every interested party that you are leaving so they can secure the place afterward. Leave the place clean and in good condition.

Since the laws and regulations covering such matters may vary from place to place, verify all of this with a local lawyer. Your area bar association offers opportunities for financially strapped individuals to consult with lawyers who are required to do a certain amount of pro bono (without charge) work.

Car Payments You Can No Longer Handle

Here's the situation: You reaffirmed your car early on, but now you wish you hadn't done that. You think it's too much car, and you know the payments are too large. What do you do now?

Three things were probably true. You were making payments, you were upside down, and you were emotionally attached to your "wheels." That may be why you made a bad decision.

You've probably thought about walking away. That's a bad idea. Don't do it. If you walk away, the finance company will repossess it and auction it off. They'll get bottom dollar for your precious wheels. They don't really care what it brings. They know they're going to get a deficiency judgment.

Since you can't go bankrupt again, they've got you where they want you. They can afford to be patient, and they will be. In the end you'll owe late fees, sale costs, legal fees, and whatever else they can get away with.

Don't wait for that to happen. Go to the lender, hat in hand. Don't ask for sympathy—this is business—instead, take them real numbers. Show them your budget and prove what you can and can't do.

Go humbly, not arrogantly. They don't owe you a break, nor do they fear what you can do to them. They have a legal right to do what they're doing. Offer to sign a note for the difference between what the car brings and what you owe.

Ask them to give you time to sell it yourself. Then find a buyer for as much as you can get. Whatever the amount, it'll be more than they would have sold it for. Since they don't really care, you can bet that no great effort will be made.

There is no perfect solution. Once you've sold the car, buy yourself a beater, and make do until you can move up a notch by paying cash. You may not look as cool, but you'll be a lot happier.

Pay the piper and be done with it. This may be a good time to consider that temporary extra job. Sell pizzas. Deliver papers. Bag groceries—whatever it takes to clean up the mess.

The Sad Truth About Co-signing

You're being asked to co-sign a note for a person close to you, someone you would like to help, and you are actually considering doing it. Would you like some advice?

Don't do it! It's a dear friend? Same advice. How about a family member? Ditto. It's one of your children? Double-don't do it! But they swear they'll pay you back, and at the time they may even mean it. They'll sound so sincere that you'll be tempted to believe them. They'll have a solid plan for paying the loan and will swear you'll never be called on to step in. They'll tell you they have money coming in—usually a tax refund, sometimes a judgment of some kind—and as soon as it comes, they swear it will be carried straight to you.

Your deck is clear. It's no surprise that someone close to you has asked you to co-sign. You already know you're a target for predatory lenders. Well, the predator who asks you to help by co-signing for them is even more dangerous, because they play the guilt card.

Here's a suggestion: quit listening to their pleas, and go watch *Judge Judy* instead. She sees a constant parade of people trying to get friends and family to do what they swore they would do.

Step back from the trap they have set for you. Leave emotion out of it. Reject guilt. This is a financial decision. Nothing more. Ignore their claim of entitlement. You don't owe anybody anything for what you have put them through, nor are they entitled to anything from you. And for goodness' sake, don't believe them about that money they'll be getting. If and when it comes, you won't know it, and when you remember to ask, it will be too late.

Listen to the experts, the professionals who lend money for a living and need to make loans in order to make a living. Don't miss that—their income depends on their making loans, and they've already said no to this person. Why? Because they've seen the financials, and they know this person cannot pay them back!

If you ignore us and co-sign anyway, sock away enough money to pay off the account yourself, because that's exactly what you'll end up doing.

Look at this as a moment of truth, one of many you will be facing. Is it going to be life as usual with yet another vicious cycle of bad decisions, or are you going to grow a backbone, plant your feet, and say, "I've had it! I'm not living like that anymore!" We hope that's what you'll do.

Getting the Best of Creditors and Collectors

Even if you never again misbehave with money, people are sometimes brought to their knees by circumstances. We want you to know how to deal with collectors and what your legal rights are regarding them.

If you borrowed money, you need to pay it back. Collectors have the right to call and ask you to do that. If they did that with class and integrity, there wouldn't be a problem.

But the bad ones—the ones we call bottom-feeders—don't have any integrity. So you need to understand what they are trying to do and how you can take care of yourself.

Start by seeing them for what they are. They aren't on your side. They could care less whether you can feed your family or keep your lights on. All they want is to be at the top of your priority list. Nothing else matters to them.

Their strategy is always the same—to make you angry or scared. They know that if you get all worked up, you will act on that emotion and do something stupid, like paying them instead of buying groceries.

They are going to sound like they're on your side, like they're your new best friend, just looking out after your interest. Expect that and look for it. Their plan is to soften you up and then spring their trap when you are vulnerable.

They are well trained. They know what to say next no matter how you respond, and what to do if that doesn't work. Don't even think about playing along or trying to outmaneuver them. They are pros. You're an amateur.

Their one and only goal is to earn their commission. You don't matter one bit. They will try anything that has ever worked, no matter how sleazy.

Your best plan, then, is to stay calm, don't believe a thing they say, remember what they're trying to do, and take pride in not letting them do it. Your failure to take the bait will drive them nuts.

Becoming Familiar with the FDCPA

The law is on your side when it comes to collectors. The Federal Fair Debt Collection Practices Act was passed in order to end some of the collectors' most unfair and nasty practices.

Here are some of the more important rules collectors are supposed to follow:

- Harassment is illegal, and repeated calls can be harassment.

- Calls can only be made between 8 a.m. and 9 p.m. your time.

- They can't call you at work if you have notified them not to.

- They can't contact third parties more than once, and then only to locate you.

- They can't discuss the details of your debt with anyone but you.

- They can't attack accounts or garnish wages without suing you.

If you are ever again contacted by collectors, you should visit the Federal Trade Commission's website or call their closest office. And don't hesitate to tell the offending collector that you're going to play that card. Sometimes that alone will bring them to a screeching halt.

Remember, if a creditor calls from the agency where your debt was discharged in the bankruptcy, he is violating federal law. Call your bankruptcy attorney immediately.

Unfortunately, you are dealing with people who have no more regard for the law than they do for your well-being. You are going to have to be both resilient and resolute.

Dealing with collectors and keeping them from making your life miserable isn't about getting out of your legitimate debt. You need to pay what you owe—but not at the expense of life's basic necessities, and most certainly not at the expense of being pushed around by professional punks who are paid only when you finally give in to their tactics.

After a lengthy search, we have identified the firm of Jacoby and Meyers as outstanding advocates for persons whose lives have been invaded by scumbag collectors who freely violate their FDCPA rights. If you have been a victim of one of these thugs, go to collectionsbully.com, and we will put you in touch with these trusted servants.

Real Questions from Real Bankruptcy Filers

Q: *If personal finance is 80 percent behavior, how do I keep from slipping back into my old behaviors? After all, I've always had them.*

A: Financially dysfunctional people are masters at self-deception. The word *denial* is still applicable. Husbands and wives must get on the same path, keep no secrets from each other, and be accountable to each other in a firm but loving way. Singles must find a trusted accountability partner. Doing it alone, in secret, and denying the reality of your situation didn't work before and it won't work now.

Q: *My wife and I both worked from the beginning. We've had separate accounts, and we've trusted each other enough not to question each other's decisions. Why can't we keep doing it that way?*

A: That's not about trust—that's about secrecy. It's about getting away with something. See it for what it is—a major red flag. If you're married, you're in this together. There is no "his debt" and "her debt," no "his account" and "her account." That may seem to work when the sun is shining, but when clouds gather, it will only lead to divisiveness, blame, and abandonment.

Q: *My spouse and I pooled our money and divided the tasks. But when things started going downhill, we both just hoped things would work themselves out. They didn't, and we were poorly prepared when the dominos started falling.*

A: That's no surprise. When you stick your head in the sand, your backside is in the perfect position to be kicked. Clarity and communication are crucial. The truth can hurt, but ignorance will destroy you. Sunlight is the best disinfectant. Do everything out in the open.

Q: *I'm getting some incredible credit card offers in the mail— some at zero percent interest. If I pay in full every month, what's wrong with having a credit card for emergencies and maybe for airline mileage?*

A: Nothing at all. There's also nothing wrong with sticking your head in a tiger's mouth if you manage to pull it out before his jaws close. Think for a minute. Why do you suppose you're getting those offers? Because they know they're likely to end up making money off of you, and they know you can't go back to the courts for relief anytime soon. Don't kid yourself—

they're not out to make you happy. They're after profit. They don't care if you get hurt in the process.

Q: I was laid off. I've been unable to find a good-paying job that uses my skills. Day after day I pound the pavement. Is it ever going to change?

A: Yes, it will change, but let's deal with the right now. Great careers have been born in the necessity of tough times. What is it you've always said you'd do if you had a choice? Well, you have one now. Remember, it's not what happens that matters. It's what you do as a result. Don't just fill out online applications, unless that's something you have to do as a required first step. Be proactive. Have a plan and a purpose. Go first to places that do what you like doing, places that will look at your experience and see that it fits their mission. Dress well and carry yourself like a winner. Show determination without being obnoxious or pushy. Try to get in front of someone who can actually make the decision. Yes, it's a battle. But the warrior wins. Be a warrior.

Q: But we need money now! How do I solve that problem?

A: Keep looking for a job, but in the meantime, look for work. There's a difference. A job is a stopping point on a career path for a period of time. Work is something you do whether you like doing it or not, as a means to an end. It's tolerable because it's temporary. Deliver pizzas at night. You can make a thousand bucks a month doing that. Deliver papers at the crack of dawn. Mow lawns or blow leaves on weekends. Clean houses. Paint houses. Fix cars. Use whatever skills and training you have. Thousands of people are doing these things, or have done them, to get ahead and win with money.

Q: What if the creditor says the debt—which I'm sure I told my lawyer about—was not discharged in my bankruptcy?

A: Don't take their word for it. Check your petition, and if it really isn't there, call your lawyer's office. If they still represent you in your bankruptcy case, they should be able to advise you how to handle this issue. There are scams out there—this may not even be a valid account. Make sure to check with your attorney first before making a deal with the creditor.

Q: What are the most important things to remember when you are trying to negotiate with a creditor, or anyone else for that matter?

A: There are several principles that deserve special emphasis. "Get it in writing" is rule one. That may seem obvious, but you'd be surprised how many people don't do it. An agreement needs to be specific about what you'll pay, when you'll pay it, and what will happen when you do pay, i.e. the entire debt is declared paid in full. Keep copies of everything you send them.

Use certified mail, return receipt requested. When the return receipt comes back, attach it to your copy. That's going to be your proof if there's ever a dispute. "Don't give anyone access to your bank account" is equally important. Doing that is like putting your family's most treasured possession in the home of a trusted friend. They might not let you down, but if they are robbed, you are out of luck. Then again, they might not be as trustworthy as you thought. That does happen, you know. While you are negotiating, insist on speaking to the same person every time, and do the same on your end. People have a strange way of not knowing, or honoring, what someone else promised. Remember that being told no does not end the negotiation. It only creates a stalemate. Be prepared to hear that word, but don't use it yourself. If you are rejecting their proposal, say, "That's not good enough." Never let anyone else decide what you can and cannot do. Just tell them that those decisions are up to you, not them.

Q: *I had to give up my car in the bankruptcy. How do I get a new car without taking out a loan?*

A: A new car is the largest investment you will ever make that tanks in value the second you drive it out of the showroom. As soon as you put miles on it, it becomes a used car. Instead, buy a good, reliable used car that you can pay for in cash right now, or save to pay for it in cash within a few months. Drive it for a year while you sock away whatever you can budget for this purpose. In a year, sell the beater—it probably hasn't lost any value—and use that money, plus what you have saved, to buy a better beater. Repeat annually until you are driving something reliable. A new car is a bad idea. Let the other guy take the depreciation beating.

Q: *I reaffirmed my house in my bankruptcy, but I have changed my mind about keeping it. What are my options?*

A: Contact your attorney first. The unwanted house poses a complex set of problems. What is the market like? What can you get for it? Are you underwater? Do you know where you and your family will go, and what that will cost? All of these questions and more should be discussed with a real estate agent—not your glad-handing brother-in-law or your cousin's neighbor who just got her license, but a superstar agent who sells more houses in your neighborhood than anyone else.

Q: *I owed taxes, student loans, and domestic support obligations prior to my bankruptcy. Do I still have to pay these?*

A: Again, contact your attorney first. The short answer is yes. In most cases, none of these three obligations can be discharged in bankruptcy. As with most things in the law, there are exceptions, so make sure to contact your attorney about the specific details of your case. The longer answer is also yes, but with a suggestion: If you owe taxes, go to the IRS with hat in hand. If you are straight with them, and your returns have been timely and accurate, they will work with you. But don't pay anyone to do that for you. That's an unnecessary expense. Do it yourself. Student loans probably cannot be negotiated. The government guarantees them, so you have no leverage. Ask anyway. It can't hurt. Child support obligations carry a lot of emotional baggage. However, there are always legal ways to ask the applicable court for relief. It's a judgment situation that can best be addressed by the lawyer who represented you in the original proceeding.

Q: *Can I get out of a residential lease, car lease, phone contract, or a gym membership contract due to my bankruptcy?*

A: Again, contact your attorney for specific legal advice. With no additional information to go on, and assuming two important facts—that you have been discharged, and that these contracts weren't listed and dealt with in your proceedings—then the answer is, probably not.

Good Advice from Quality Counsel in the Trenches

Emory Clark and Rich Thompson of Clark & Washington

Most lenders offering easy credit after bankruptcy are going to hit you with exorbitant fees, high interest rates, even higher default rates, and cascading defaults.

America's concept of keeping money aside for a rainy day has drastically changed for the worse. The first goal after a bankruptcy discharge should not be to establish new debt; it should be to establish and fund a meaningful savings vehicle.

Jim Coutinho of Strip, Hoppers, Leithart, McGrath & Terlecky

You've been through some rough times. No one likes filing bankruptcy, and it can be hard coming to terms with it. Forgive yourself. Beating yourself up is a waste of energy and time. Forgive yourself and start the process of building something better.

People like to refer to bankruptcy as a fresh start. I like to call it a do-over. It's a chance to rethink your life, to reinvent your finances, and to learn from your mistakes. Take advantage of that chance. Act on that opportunity.

Bankruptcy may not relieve you of all debts. You may have a mortgage, student loans, car payments, etc. You still have a lot to do to be financially healthy. Educate yourself about the right way, and clean up what mess you have left.

Christine Wilton of the Law Office of Christine A. Wilton

Seek advice from professionals, but never let them make the decision for you. Learn from those who have been there, and make your own well-informed decisions.

Spend less than you make. Paying yourself first means saving for retirement. Don't worry about what your neighbors are doing, because you now have a plan and support from professionals to guide you.

Jim Ince of Bailey & Galyen

Check your credit report a few months after filing bankruptcy to see if it shows the proper debts discharged. Quickly challenge it if it does not. If correct, it limits the ability of the creditor to sell the debt, which could save a lot of future headaches.

Always keep copies of your original paperwork and discharge order, and put them where you can get to them. That can save you hours of time in the future.

John Newton of Mayer & Newton

Most of our clients ask about credit scores before they file bankruptcy. It is very important to them how the bankruptcy itself will affect their credit score. If a debt has been reaffirmed, check your credit report regularly to make sure payments are being posted accurately. It is not a good idea to incur new debts or to act irresponsibly. Good luck.

Bob Harlan of Harlan & Associates

Watch out for mortgage companies who try to collect bogus arrearages on continuing home mortgage payments. Often clients don't know exactly which month's payments the trustee paid, so they accept the faulty accounting and pay the overcharges without question.

Something like one-third of all securitized mortgages (those with hired servicing companies) overcharge customers within six months after discharge in the form of bogus late fees and inspection charges or insurance that was not necessary.

Double charging for insurance occurs when clients have their own, but the premium notice suggests cancellation, so the mortgage company imposes a year's worth of insurance premiums to an affiliated insurance company.

The only way you can get the full accounting from your mortgage company is with a Qualified Written Request (QWR) through RESPA. Be sure your lawyer does that.

Erin B. Shank, Attorney at Law ———————————————

After the client's case is discharged, they should send a letter to each of the three credit bureaus informing them of the discharge and including a copy of the discharge and the listing of the debts discharged. The letter should request the three credit bureaus to show that all of the debts on the court's discharge order have in fact been discharged. They should also ask the credit bureaus to send a corrected copy of the client's credit bureau report to the client. This process will clean up their credit record.

Notes

1. Mike Ransdell, "Buyer Beware," *Carnegie Mellon Today*, June 2007, Volume 4, Number 2.

2. Herb Weisbaum, "We spend grubby bills and keep the crisp ones," Life Inc., November 14, 2012, http://lifeinc.today.com/_news/2012/11/14/15167761-we-spend-grubby-bills-and-keep-the-crisp-ones?lite.

3. Alexis Leondis, "Cardholders Prefer Debit as Credit-Card Use Falls," Bloomberg, September 8, 2010, http://www.bloomberg.com/news/2010-09-08/cardholders-prefer-debit-as-credit-card-use-falls-javelin-says.html.

4. Dan Kadlec, "How to Save $2,500 a Year on Lunch," *TIME* Business & Money, August 29, 2012, http://business.time.com/2012/08/29/how-to-save-2500-a-year-on-lunch/.

5. Jon Acuff, *Quitter: Closing the Gap Between Your Day Job and Your Dream Job* (Nashville: Lampo Press, 2011), 68.

6. Brian Dakss, "4 In 5 Credit Reports Have Errors," CBS News, February 11, 2009, http://www.cbsnews.com/2100-500200_162-648887.html.

7. "Retirement in America," 2002 Retirement Confidence Survey, EBRI/ASEC/Greenwald, http://www.ebri.org/pdf/surveys/rcs/2002/riafs.pdf.

8. 2011 Data Breach Stats, Identity Theft Resource Center, December 27, 2011, http://www.idtheftcenter.org/ITRC%20Breach%20Stats%20Report%202011.pdf.

9. Marcie Geffner, "Why a home equity loan is hard to get," Bankrate.com, January 31, 2011, http://www.bankrate.com/finance/home-equity/why-a-home-equity-loan-is-hard-to-get.aspx.